Special Days

Holidays and Celebrations

by Emily C. Dawson

amicus readers 1

Amicus Readers are published by Amicus
P.O. Box 1329, Mankato, Minnesota 56002

Printed in the United States of America at Corporate Graphics, North Mankato, Minnesota.

Library of Congress Cataloging-in-Publication Data
Dawson, Emily C.
  Holidays and celebrations / by Emily C. Dawson.
      p. cm. – (Amicus readers. Special days)
  Includes index.
  Summary: "Describes common holidays and celebrations such as graduation, and how people celebrate these special days. Includes simple craft"–Provided by publisher.
  ISBN 978-1-60753-030-5 (library binding)
  1. Holidays–United States–Juvenile literature. 2. Festivals–United States–Juvenile literature. 3. United States–Social life and customs–Juvenile literature. I. Title.
  GT4803.A2D42 2011
  394.26973–dc22

                                                    2010009108

Series Editor   Rebecca Glaser
Series Designer   Emily Brown
Book Designer   Heather Dreisbach
Photo Researcher   Heather Dreisbach

Photo Credits
Ariel Skelley/Getty Images, cover; Corbis/Tranz, 7, 20 (graduates); Dreamstime, 9, 21 (fireworks); Gino Santa Maria/iStockphoto, 3, 20–24 (fireworks); Nicole S. Young/iStockphoto, 15, 21 (boy in cemetery); PhotoBliss/Alamy, 19, 20 (children in parade); Photodisc, 5, 11, 20 (birthday party), 21 (wedding); Richard Schultz/Getty Images, 1, 13, 20 (trick-or-treaters); Yellow Dog Productions/Getty Images, 17, 21 (family gathering)

1225
42010

10 9 8 7 6 5 4 3 2 1

Table of Contents

A year is filled
with holidays
and celebrations.

Sarah's birthday is
in March. She invited
five friends to her party.

In May, Dan
and his friends
celebrate graduation.

They are happy
to be done with
high school.

July 4 is Independence Day. This is the day the United States became a country.

Emily's family watches fireworks.

In August, David and Rosa get married.

Weddings can happen any time of year.

Thanksgiving is
in November, too.

Ava visits
her uncle.

Her mom brings
a pie to share.

The year starts again.

Mai and Ling walk
in a Chinese New
Year parade.

What holidays and
special days does
your family celebrate?

Picture Glossary

birthday

the day a person was born, celebrated each year

Chinese New Year

a holiday that celebrates the start of the new year based on the Chinese calendar

graduation

the day students get a diploma saying they have completed the last year in a school

Halloween

a holiday celebrated at the end of October, when kids dress up in costumes

Independence Day

a U.S. holiday celebrated on July 4th; it is the day the United States became a country.

Thanksgiving

a U.S. holiday that celebrates the Pilgrims' first harvest feast

Veterans Day

a holiday when we honor those who have fought in wars and served in the armed forces

wedding

a ceremony when two people get married, or agree to live their lives together

Make a Calendar

Supplies:

- Computer and printer
- Construction paper
- Glue
- Markers or stickers
- Stapler

1. Print calendar pages from a calendar software program or from the Internet. Go to: www.dltk-cards.com/calendar/

2. Glue calendar pages onto construction paper.

3. Use markers or stickers to mark birthdays and holidays on the calendar.

4. Staple all the months together in order. Hang your calendar on the wall.

Ideas for Parents and Teachers

Special Days, an Amicus Readers Level 1 series, gives children practice reading about common celebrations. The picture glossary reinforces new vocabulary. The activities give children a chance to apply what they have learned. Use the ideas below to help children get even more out of their reading experience.

Before Reading:

- Ask the children what holidays they celebrate.
- Ask them about other occasions when they might have a party.
- Look at the picture glossary words. Tell children to watch for them as they read the book.

Read the Book:

- Read the book to the children or have them read independently.
- Show children how to use the features of the book such as the glossary and web sites.

After Reading:

- Invite the students to choose one special occasion and compare the photos in the book to how they celebrate it. Have them share what they do.
- Make a chart with two columns, holidays and celebrations. Have the children sort the things in the book into each column. Explain that everyone celebrates holidays, while other occasions are celebrated with only family and friends.
- Review the months of the year. Start with the months in the book. Then ask the children to name holidays that happen in other months.

Index

Web Sites

Kids Holiday Crafts: Home
http://www.kidsholidaycrafts.com/

Kids' Turn Central—Holidays
http://www.kidsturncentral.com/holidays.htm

PBS Kids: Halloween
http://pbskids.org/halloween/